How To Create An App

Author: Duong Tran
Cover and Text by Duong Tran

Copyright: This book is a registered product. It is intended to be accurate. All Products, logos, and brands are trademarks of their respective owners. Thank you for supporting by purchasing a copy of this book.

About the Author: I am also the author of my other books: Information Technology 2016, Network System Administration 2016, Cloud and Data Center, Information Technology Handbook, and Network and System Administration Handbook. In 2016, I made some money about $500 for selling IT Books. That was enough to buy diapers last year. Thank you for supporting my IT books as well.

Introduction: My philosophy is that if a person can play a mobile game, the person can create a game. It is fun to start to create an app first. Later, the person can create a game. Mobile app developer salary is one of the highest paying jobs too. This book is fast and easy to learn. Let start how to create a mobile app for iPhone, Android, and Windows Phone.

List of Contents

Mobile App Developer @Salary.com

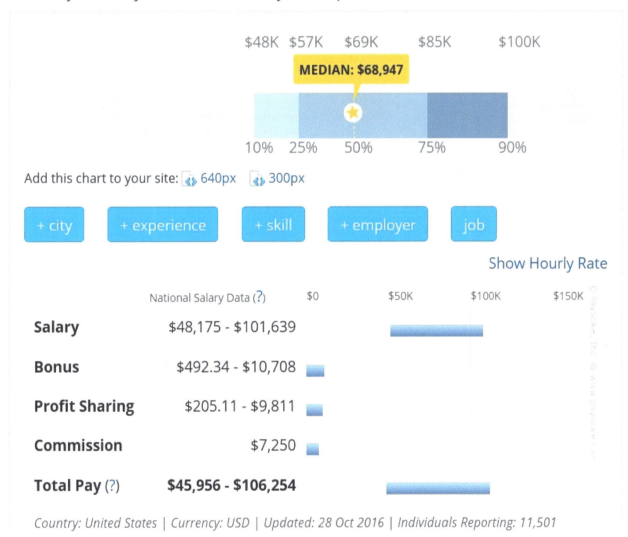

Software developers has an average salary of $68K compared to mobile app $97K in the U.S.A. It is one of the highest paying job.

Mobile Apple Developer @VisionMobile

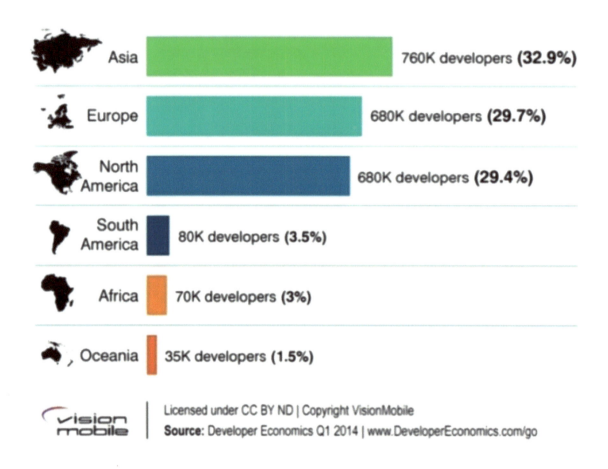

Source: *VisionMobile*

There are about 680K mobile developers in North America. The big three Asia, Europe and North America have the total over two millions (2,200,000) mobile developers. The industry is hiring a lot of mobile developers world wide.

Mobile App Development flow @cestarcollege.com

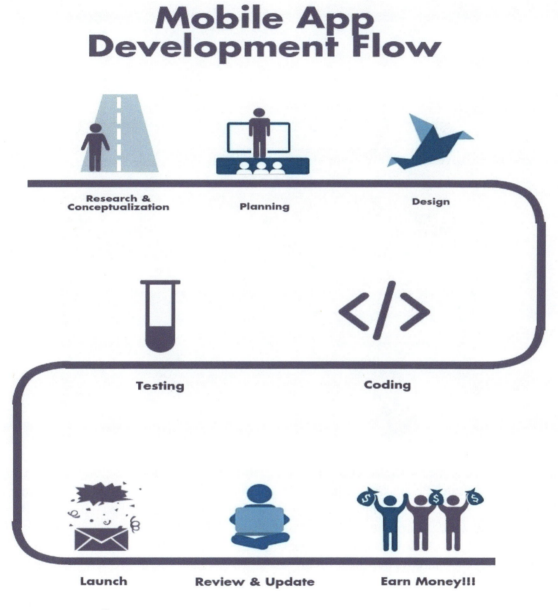

www.cestarcollege.com

To start a mobile app, do some research first. Next, plans for the time. How to code? Which programming language? How to test using the emulator? Do some testings like user testing. Publish the app to stores and marketing.

Mobile Architecture

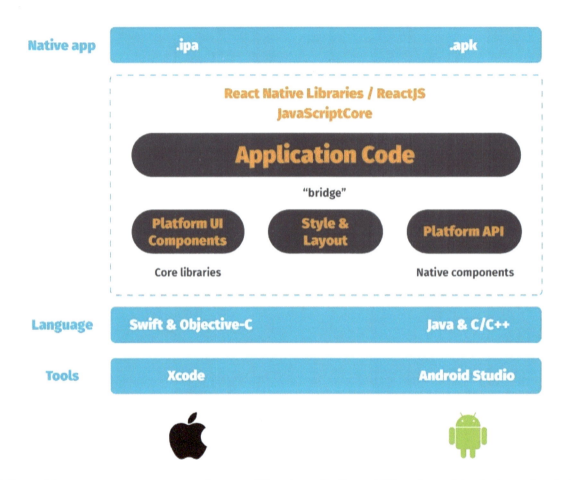

Mobile architecture components are the core libraries, platform API and graphic design. Apple Xcode is a developer tool to create iPhone app. It includes the compiler and swift programming language. The swift programming is based on Objective-C. iOS application packages are saved in the .ipa. Android Studio is another developer tool to create mobile app for Android devices with Java and C/C++ programming languages. Android application packages are saved in the zip file.apk. Microsoft introduced the Universal Windows Platform for all Windows devices based on .NET architecture. Microsoft also invested in Xamarin, a company that created a cross platform for iPhone/Android/Windows.

Mobile Architecture @Microsoft.com

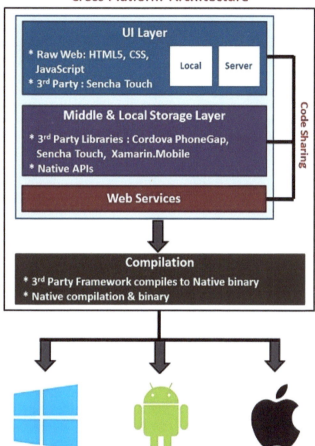

HTML5, CSS, JavaScript are web programming languages and code shared that the app is using the web service to connect to app server or game server which allows multi players and messaging. It is difference than a standard or tradition game that the user downloads to the device and plays alone.

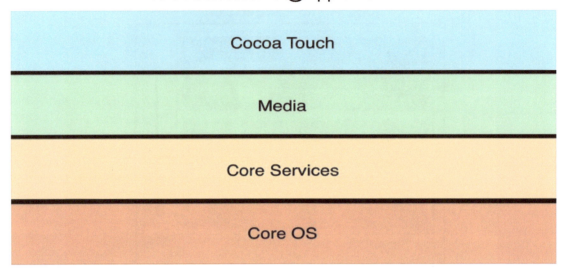

iOS Architecture @Apple.com

Cocoa Touch supports the appearing of the screen like the AirDrop Framework which allows to share photos and documents. The TexKit Framework supports text control. UIKit Framework supports the behaviors of the objects. Address Book UI Framework allows to manage contact information. EvenKit Frameworks allows to add/edit/view calendar events. GameKit Framework supports gaming. iAD Framework allows to add advertise banner to the game. MapKit Frameworks provides map direction for the app. Message UI Framework provides messaging. Notification Framwork provides display information. PushKit Framework alerts incoming call for the app.

Media provides core graphic, audio, and video frameworks. Core Audio Frameworks are a set of frameworks to manage audio. Core Graphic Frameworks provide graphic. Core Image Frameworks provide images Core Text Frameworks provide text layout. Core Video Frameworks provide video. Other media frameworks are Game Controller Frameworks, Image I/O Frameworks, Media Accessibility Framework, Media Player Frameworks, Metal Frameworks, OpenAL Framework, OpenGL ES Framework, Photo Frameworks, Photo UI Framework, Quartz Framework, SceneKit Framework and SpriteKit Framework.

Core Services provide system services like iCloud, social media, and networking from the CloudKit Framework, Social Framework, CFNetwork Framework, Core Data Framework, Account Framework, Address Book Framework, AD Support Framework, Core Location Framework, Core Media Framework, Core Motion Framework, Core Telephony Framewor, EvenKit Framework, HealthKit Framework, HomeKit Frameowrk, JavaScript Core Framework, Mobile Core Service Framework, Multi Peer Connectivity Framework, NewstandKit Framework, PassKit Framework, QuickLook Framework, Safari Service Framework, StoreKit Framework, Core Foundation Framework, System Configuration Framework and WebKit.

Core OS provides Generic Security Services Framework, External Accessory Framework, Local Authentication Framework, Network Extension Frameworks, Security Framework and System drivers

The iOS Architecture @Apple.com

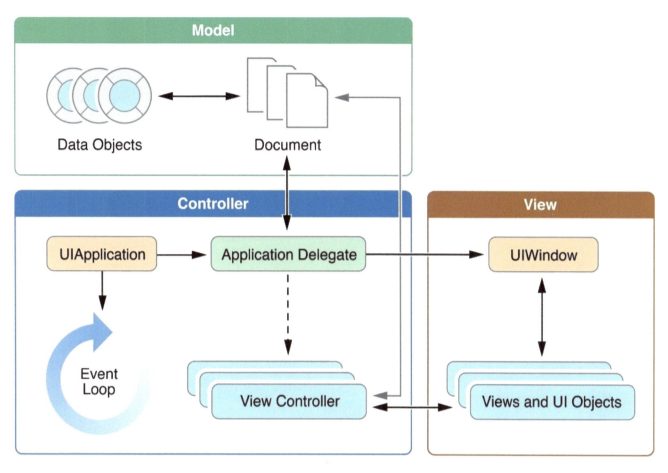

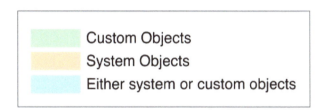

iOS apps are based on Model-View-Control architecture. In the View, the UIWindow object display the contents, windows, graphic layout, and user interface. The Controller manages how to display the View. The UIApplication object in the Controller sends the event or events to the View Controller and to the View. During the process, the app accesses the data and document from the Model. Another way to easy understand is View-Control-Model. It should be called View-Control-Data. However, the Data has its model. Anyway, the iOS apps or games are based on Model-View-Control processes.

Xcode @Apple.com

Welcome to Xcode

No Recent Projects

 Get started with a playground
Explore new ideas quickly and easily.

 Create a new Xcode project
Create an app for iPhone, iPad, Mac, Apple Watch or Apple TV.

 Check out an existing project
Start working on something from an SCM repository.

☑ Show this window when Xcode launches   Open another project...

Xcode 8 is the latest version built-in Swift 3 programming language. It is a compiler and interface builder. It requires Apple macOS computer. It can be downloaded at https://developer.apple.com/xcode/

Xcode @Apple.com

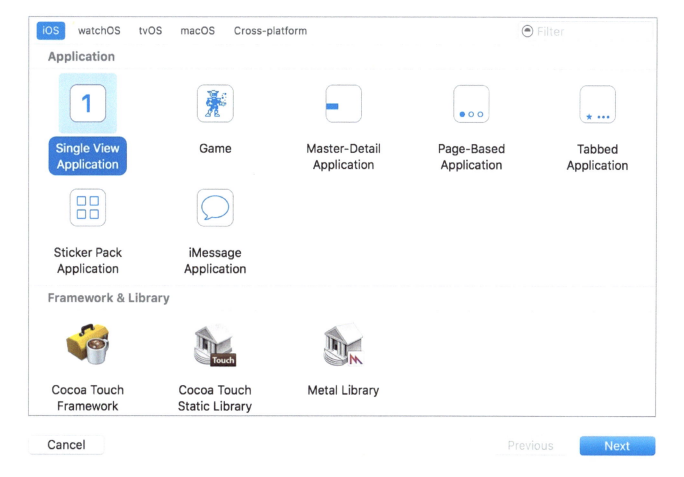

Open Xcode and choose iOS, there are some templates ready. Click on Single View Application.

Xcode @Apple.com

Choose options for your new project:

Product Name:	FoodTracker
Team:	None
Organization Name:	Apple Inc.
Organization Identifier:	com.example
Bundle Identifier:	com.example.FoodTracker
Language:	Swift
Devices:	Universal

☐ Use Core Data
☑ Include Unit Tests
☐ Include UI Tests

Cancel   Previous   Next

Name the app and the team. Choose Swift. Choose the device. Select Include Unit Tests and Include UI Tests. If Core Data is used, select Core Data. Otherwise, leave it blank.

Xcode @Apple.com

Toolbar

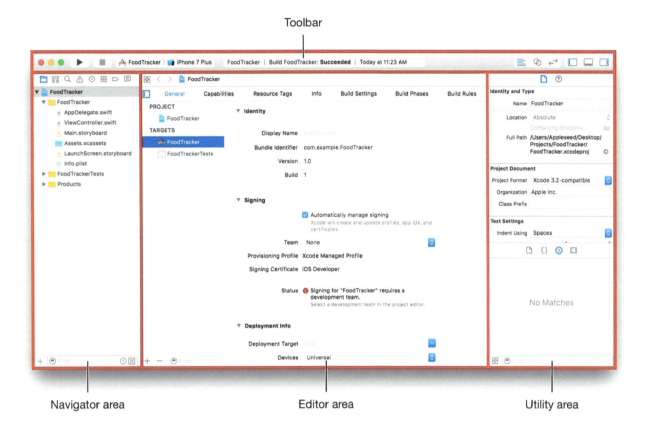

Navigator area   Editor area   Utility area

Xcode has four areas: Toolbar tabs with the emulator functions for testing devices, the Navigator area project structure, the Editor area for work space, the Utility area for settings.

Xcode @Apple.com

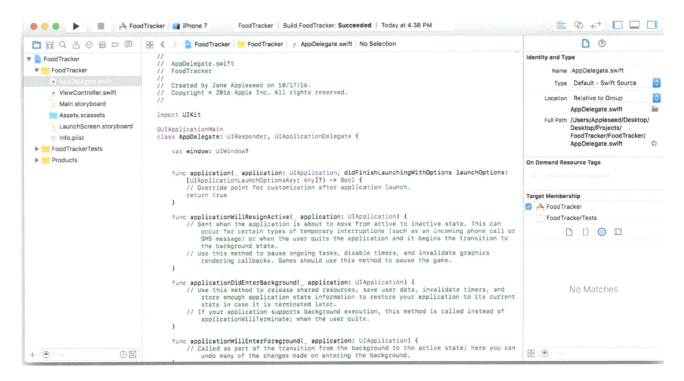

The AppDelegate.swift is the source code file. The actual binary file is the .app file. The ViewController.swift is another source code file to control the displays. The Main.storyboard is the interface builder. The Asseets.xassets contains resource files such as images. The Test folder contains test activities. If this is a framework folder, the folder contains plug-in frameworks. Another folder can be added to store the resource files. The Products folder contains the executable file .app. The native project is saved as the .ipa archive compressed file. The .ipa file structure contains the .app file, the metadata .plist file, and other app data. Objective-C programming language uses the .h and .m files for header and object implementation.

Swift language is based on C and Objective-C created by Apple. Swift includes compiler, standard library, SDK overlay and debugger. The swift file is the source file. It takes times to learn the swift programming. Many open sources and commercial frameworks are available to create mobile app quickly with no code or less coding required.

Android Architecture @Android.com

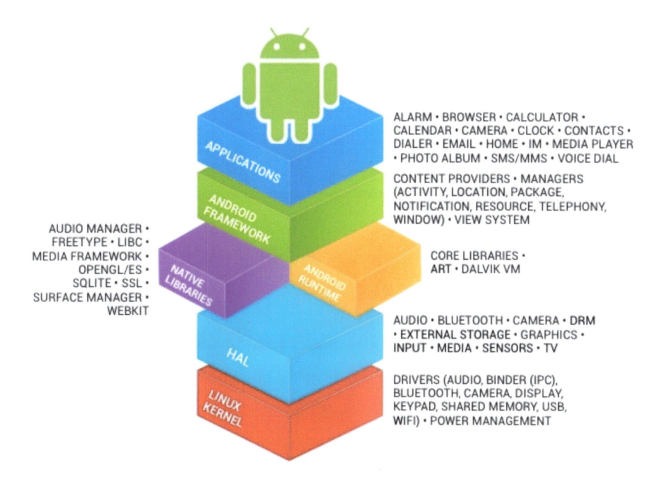

Android architecture is built on Linux Kernel. Android app cores are Android Framework, Android Runtime (Android RunTime ART and DALVIK Virtual Machine), and Native Libraries (Web engine WebKIT, 3D Graphic Libary OPENGL/ES, SQLite database, Secure Sockets Layer SSL,.etc). Android supports C/C++/Java and allows other run-times plug-in to create C# app, HTML5 and other programming languages. This means Android is an open source.

Android Architecture @Android.com

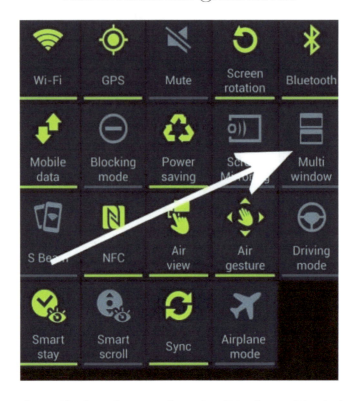

Android 7 is the latest version. The best feature of version 7 is the multi-windows.

Android Architecture @Xamarin.com

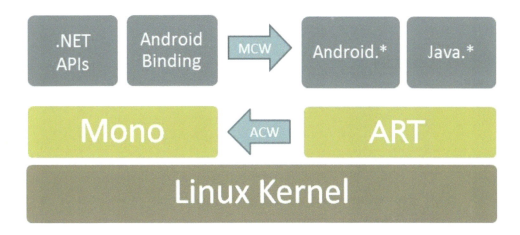

The .NET APIs use Mono runtime because it was written in C language. The Java APIs use the Android Runtime because the Android Runtime was written in Java language. Android Architecture supports both environments.

Android Studio @Android.com

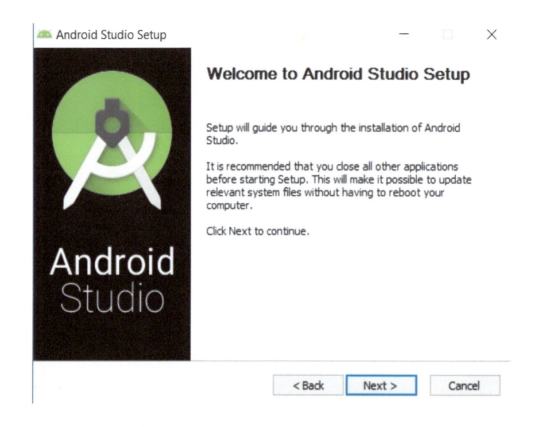

Android Studio cores are Android app modules, Library modules, Google App Engine modules. Download Android Studio @ https://developer.android.com/studio/index.html

Android Studio

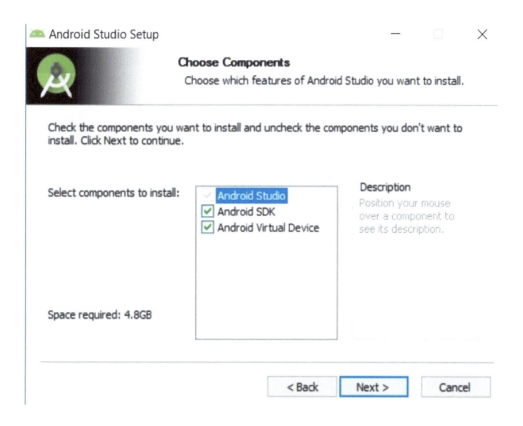

Other than the cores, the other components are the Android SDK Software Development Kit and the Android Virtual Device. Click Next and Next to complete the installation. It takes a few minutes for the installation.

Android Studio

Welcome to Android Studio   —   □   ✕

Android Studio

Version 2.2.3

☀ Start a new Android Studio project

📁 Open an existing Android Studio project

⬇ Check out project from Version Control ▾

📥 Import project (Eclipse ADT, Gradle, etc.)

📥 Import an Android code sample

⚙ Configure ▾   Get Help ▾

Android Studio 2.2.3 is the latest version

Android Studio

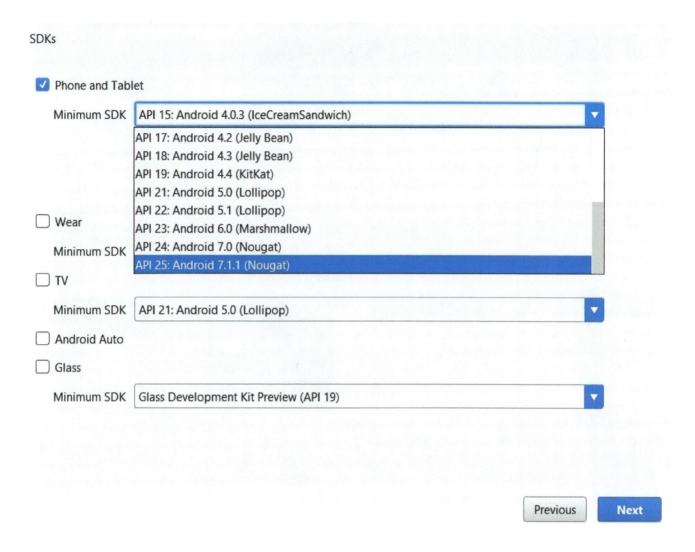

Scroll down to select Android 7.1.1

Android Studio

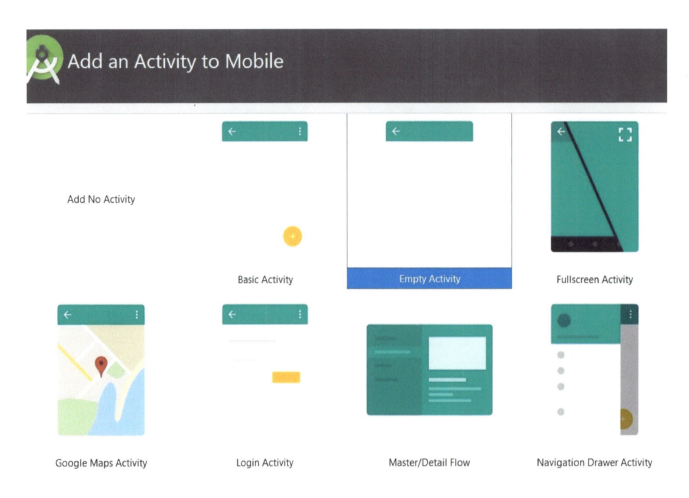

Select Empty Activity to create a blank project.

Android Studio

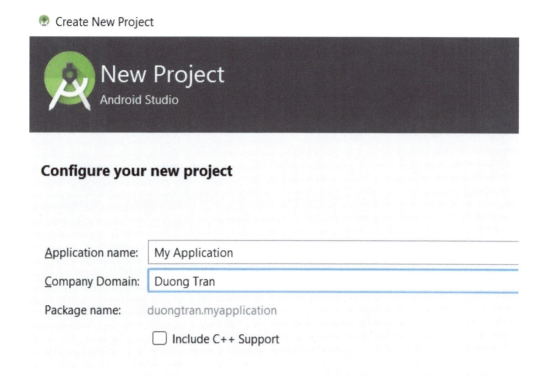

Name the app and an individual/organization.

Android Studio

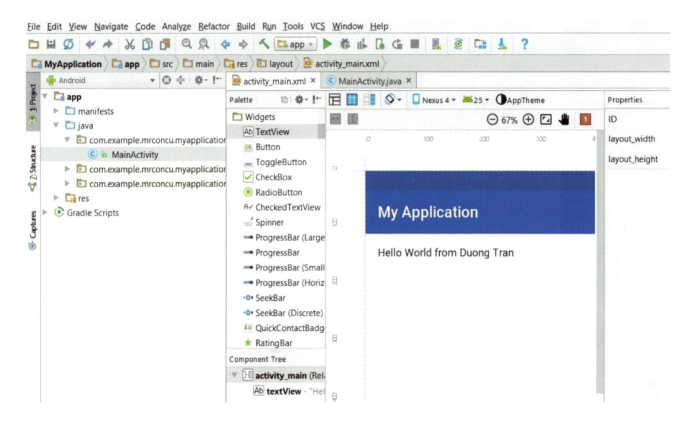

Click on the MainActivity and design the app.

Android Studio

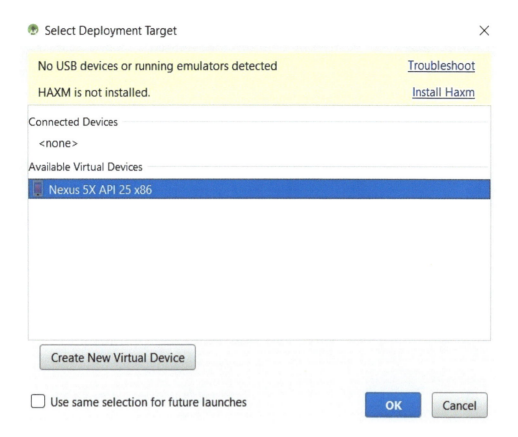

Select or create a new virtual device to run the app.

Android Studio

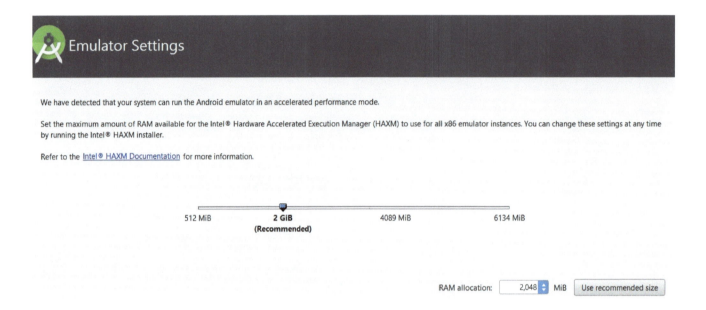

Set the virtual RAM for the simulator. It is actually used the real computer RAM.

Android Studio

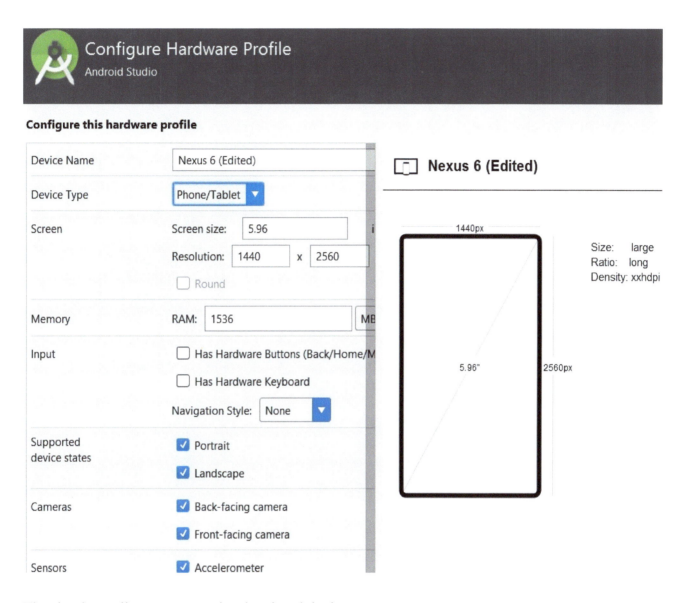

The simulator allows to customize the virtual devices.

Android Studio

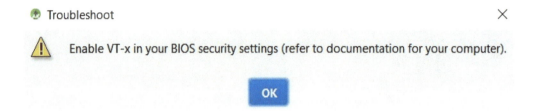

The emulator requires to restart the computer to changes the BIOS setting for the hardware chip to enable virtual technology chip. Shutdown the computer, power on, press F10 (for most computers) to enter the BIOS. In the System setting, enable Virtualization Technology, Save and Exit. Open Android Studio, another screen will pop-up to notify that Android will disable Hyper-V to use the emulator.

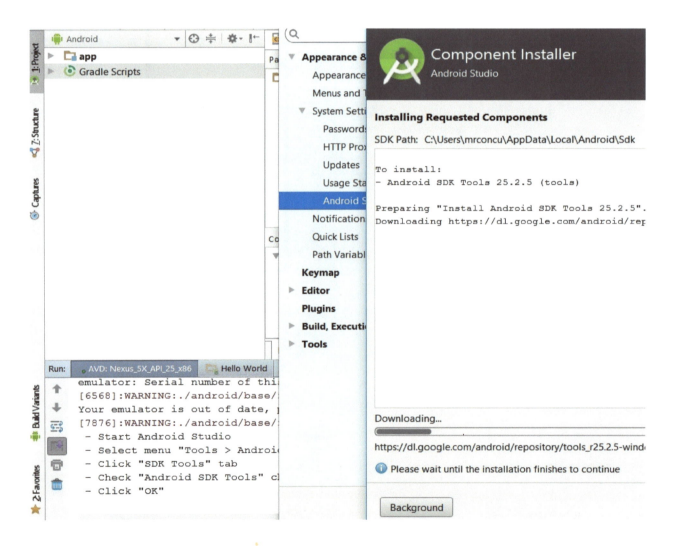

An update is required. It displays on the top right menu or running the emulator.

Android Studio

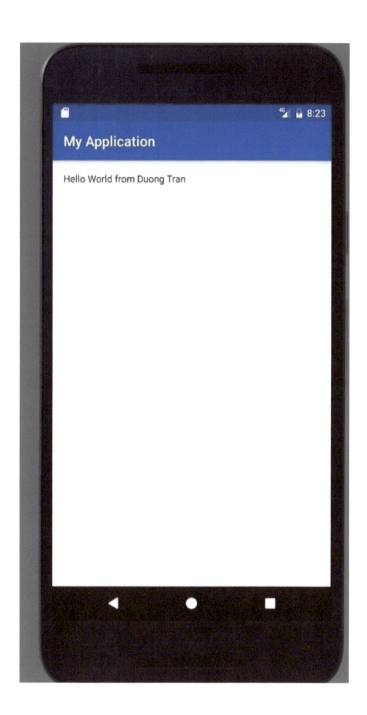

Run the app, the virtual phone will pop-up.

Universal Windows Platform @Microsoft.com

1

Microsoft Universal Windows Platform UWP is a run-time for Windows 10 Mobile and Windows 10 devices. It supports C++, C#, F#, VB.NET, XAML and JavaScript. Visual Studio 2015 is included UWP. Visual Studio 2015 is also included the Xamarin to develop Andriod and iOS apps.

1

Universal Windows Platform @Microsoft.com

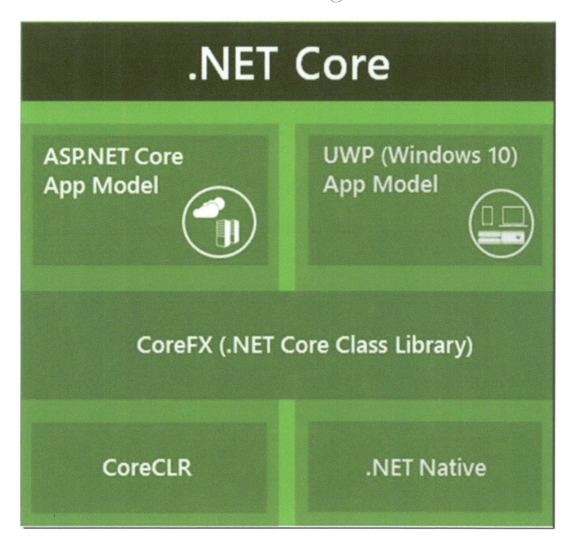

The UWP uses the .NET Core Class Library.

Universal Windows Platform @Microsoft.com

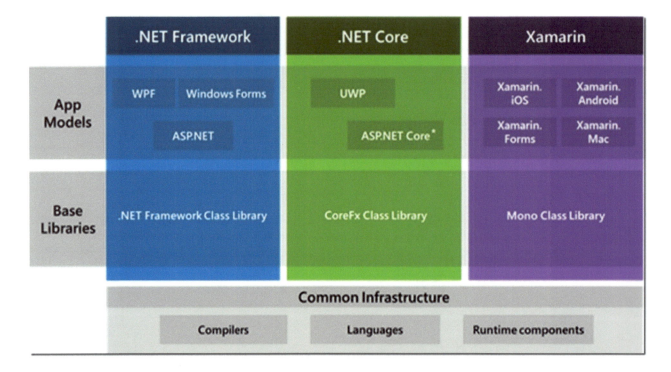

The original .NET Framework uses the .NET Framework Class Library. The UWP uses the CoreFx Class Library. Xamarin uses the Mono Class Library. Apps may be written in common compilers, languages, or Runtime. Microsoft adds all three together to make a big tool to use in Visual Studio. Big means many gigabytes package to download and times to install. The default installation takes about 36 GB. It also needs many more available disk space for updates, plug-in, emulator, apps. It is recommended to have a great computer with a lot of memory.

Visual Studio

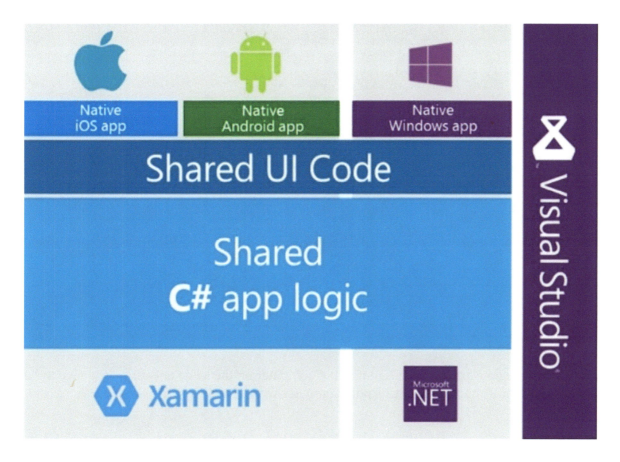

Xamarin add-on for Visual Studio allows multiple devices to use the same code C#. It includes multiple simulators.

Visual Studio @Xamarin.com

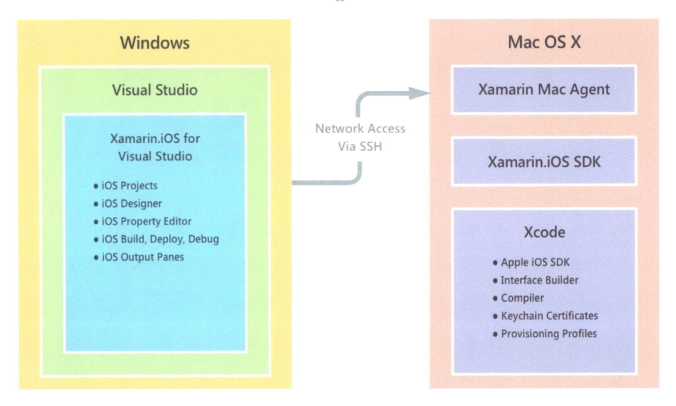

For Cross Platform, add Xamarin Mac Agent to the computer on the same network. It is nice to have an Apple computer or try to run a virtual Apple computer with VirtualBox.

Visual Studio

Xamarin and Visual Studio web installation is available @Xamarin.com. By default, Visual C++ Tool, Universal Window App Development Tool, Cross Platform Mobile Development C#/.NET, Android Native Development Kit(s), Android SDK and Java Development Kit are selected to install. Some others are not selected like the Visual C++ Mobile Development and HTML/JavaScript Apache Cordova.

Visual Studio

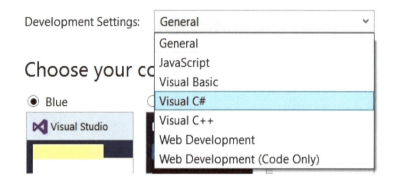

You can always change these settings later.

Start Visual Studio

Open Visual Studio 2015, choose a programming language.

Visual Studio

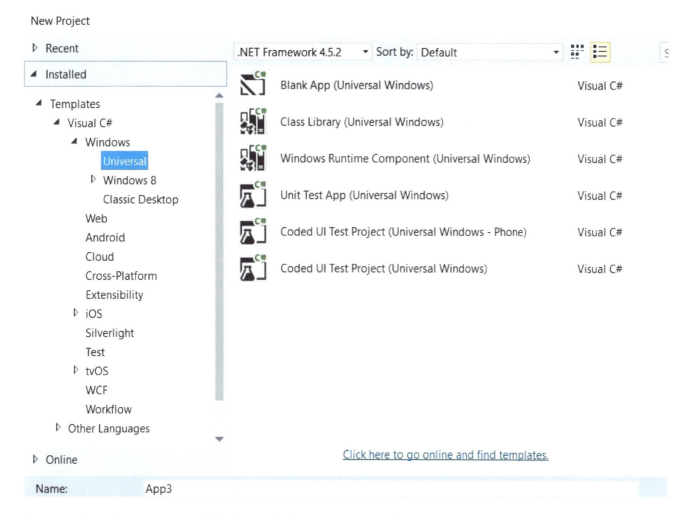

Create a New Project, select Windows, Universal, and Blank App (Universal Windows)

Visual Studio

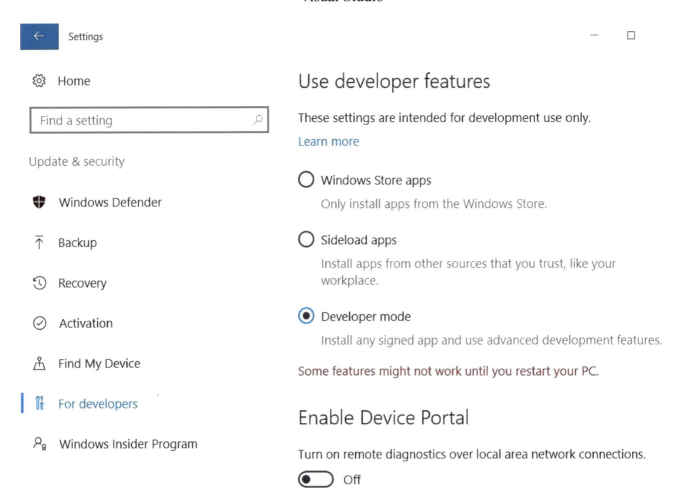

Turn on Developer mode to use the UI design in Visual Studio 2015

Visual Studio

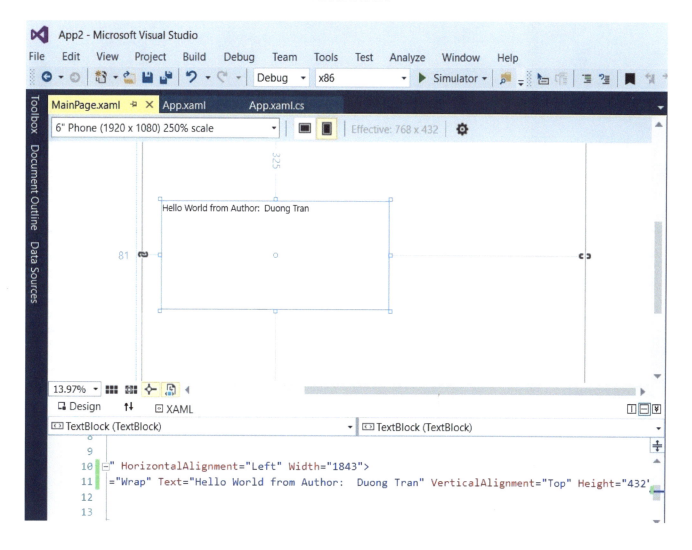

On the top left corner, Select a Windows Phone, design the interface and run the simulator.

Visual Studio

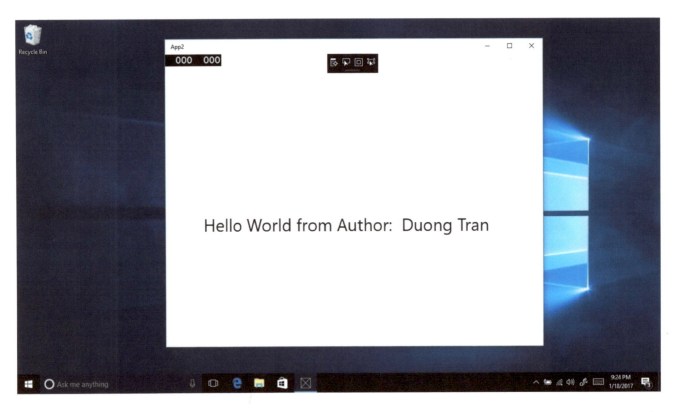

The app is running. Do not do anything wrong with the simulator other than running the app because it affects the computer.

Visual Studio

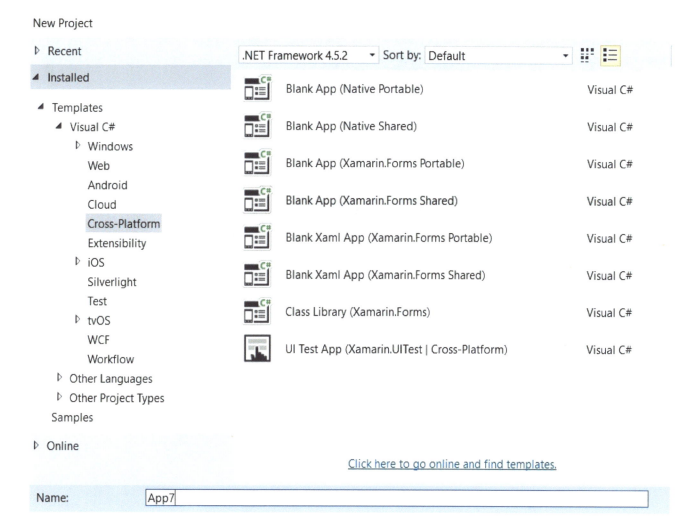

To create a shared app cross-platform for team work, open the Visual Studio and create a new project, then select Cross-Platform and select a shared template.

Visual Studio

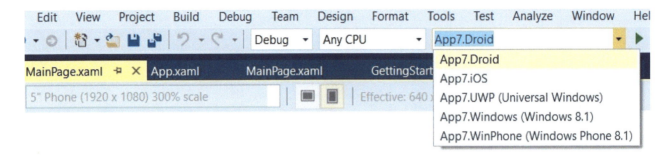

Cross Platform Shared Project has multiple simulators. For iOS, it requires MAC OS computer. Alternately, The developer can try VirtualBox to run MAC OS and Xcode, but it is outside the scope of this book.

Visual Studio

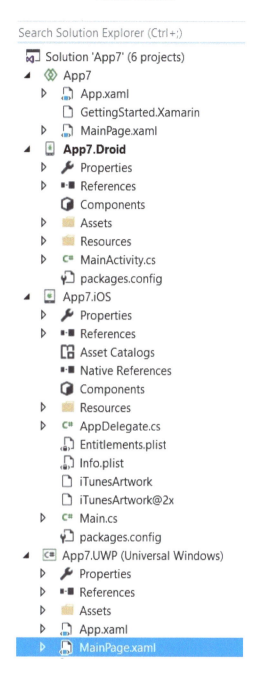

Solution Explorer Bar displays all App.Droid, App.iOS, and App.UWP shared project files.

Words from Author

Now, you know how to create an app. It is fun to design and create your own app. You can become a mobile developer.

Thank you for buying my book. I am looking into to create the second book. Please leave a positive comment and rating. Do not read any book one time, keep it.

Duong Tran